Parks and Recreation

MAD LIBS®

by Alexandra L. Wolfe

MAD LIBS
An Imprint of Penguin Random House LLC, New York

Mad Libs format copyright © 2021 by Penguin Random House LLC.
All rights reserved.

Concept created by Roger Price & Leonard Stern

Parks and Recreation © 2021 Universal Television LLC. All Rights Reserved.

Published by Mad Libs,
an imprint of Penguin Random House LLC, New York.
Printed in the USA.

Visit us online at www.penguinrandomhouse.com.

ISBN 9780593226766
1 3 5 7 9 10 8 6 4 2

MAD LIBS®

INSTRUCTIONS

MAD LIBS® is a game for people who don't like games! It can be played by one, two, three, four, or forty.

• RIDICULOUSLY SIMPLE DIRECTIONS

In this tablet you will find stories containing blank spaces where words are left out. One player, the READER, selects one of these stories. The READER does not tell anyone what the story is about. Instead, he/she asks the other players, the WRITERS, to give him/her words. These words are used to fill in the blank spaces in the story.

• TO PLAY

The READER asks each WRITER in turn to call out a word—an adjective or a noun or whatever the space calls for—and uses them to fill in the blank spaces in the story. The result is a MAD LIBS® game.

When the READER then reads the completed MAD LIBS® game to the other players, they will discover that they have written a story that is fantastic, screamingly funny, shocking, silly, crazy, or just plain dumb—depending upon which words each WRITER called out.

• EXAMPLE (*Before* and *After*)

"_____!" he said _____
        EXCLAMATION   ADVERB

as he jumped into his convertible _____ and
                                                    NOUN

drove off with his _____ wife.
                            ADJECTIVE

"_____OUCH_____!" he said _____HAPPILY_____
        EXCLAMATION   ADVERB

as he jumped into his convertible _____CAT_____ and
                                                    NOUN

drove off with his _____BRAVE_____ wife.
                            ADJECTIVE

MAD☺LIBS®
QUICK REVIEW

In case you have forgotten what adjectives, adverbs, nouns, and verbs are, here is a quick review:

An ADJECTIVE describes something or somebody. *Lumpy, soft, ugly, messy,* and *short* are adjectives.

An ADVERB tells how something is done. It modifies a verb and usually ends in "ly." *Modestly, stupidly, greedily,* and *carefully* are adverbs.

A NOUN is the name of a person, place, or thing. *Sidewalk, umbrella, bridle, bathtub,* and *nose* are nouns.

A VERB is an action word. *Run, pitch, jump,* and *swim* are verbs. Put the verbs in past tense if the directions say PAST TENSE. *Ran, pitched, jumped,* and *swam* are verbs in the past tense.

When we ask for A PLACE, we mean any sort of place: a country or city (*Spain, Cleveland*) or a room (*bathroom, kitchen*).

An EXCLAMATION or SILLY WORD is any sort of funny sound, gasp, grunt, or outcry, like *Wow!, Ouch!, Whomp!, Ick!,* and *Gadzooks!*

When we ask for specific words, like a NUMBER, a COLOR, an ANIMAL, or a PART OF THE BODY, we mean a word that is one of those things, like *seven, blue, horse,* or *head.*

When we ask for a PLURAL, it means more than one. For example, *cat* pluralized is *cats.*

MAD LIBS® is fun to play with friends, but you can also play it by yourself! To begin with, DO NOT look at the story on the page below. Fill in the blanks on this page with the words called for. Then, using the words you have selected, fill in the blank spaces in the story.

Now you've created your own hilarious MAD LIBS® game!

WELCOME TO PAWNEE!

ADJECTIVE _____

FIRST NAME _____

CITY _____

COUNTRY _____

VERB _____

PLURAL NOUN _____

LETTER OF THE ALPHABET _____

TYPE OF FOOD (PLURAL) _____

ADJECTIVE _____

ADJECTIVE _____

PLURAL NOUN _____

VERB ENDING IN "ING" _____

TYPE OF BUILDING _____

NOUN _____

VERB _____

NOUN _____

OCCUPATION (PLURAL) _____

ANIMAL _____

WELCOME TO PAWNEE!

Welcome to Pawnee, Indiana, the most _____ place in the
ADJECTIVE
world! Well, at least I, _____ Knope, think it is. I even
FIRST NAME
wrote a book about it—_____ : *The Greatest Town in*
CITY
_____ . Here in Pawnee, there are so many statues to
COUNTRY
_____ and leafy _____ to see. But don't miss
VERB   PLURAL NOUN
J-_____ 's Diner, home of their world-famous
LETTER OF THE ALPHABET
_____ . Then, check out our many _____
TYPE OF FOOD (PLURAL)   ADJECTIVE
parks, like the Pawnee Commons and Indiana's smallest park. Those
two have a/an _____ place in my heart. Speaking of parks,
ADJECTIVE
no tour would be complete without checking out City Hall, which is
where I work in the _____ and Recreation Department.
PLURAL NOUN
Sure, people also seem to like _____ in the Wamapoke
VERB ENDING IN "ING"
Casino, the Sweetums _____, or the Snakehole
TYPE OF BUILDING
_____ , but wouldn't you rather watch democracy
NOUN
_____ instead? No matter where you go, Pawnee has a/an
VERB
_____ for everyone. Just steer clear of Eagleton—only rich,
NOUN
snobby _____ live in _____ -ton!
OCCUPATION (PLURAL)   ANIMAL

MAD LIBS® is fun to play with friends, but you can also play it by yourself! To begin with, DO NOT look at the story on the page below. Fill in the blanks on this page with the words called for. Then, using the words you have selected, fill in the blank spaces in the story.

Now you've created your own hilarious MAD LIBS® game!

LESLIE AND BEN 4EVER

VERB _____

ADJECTIVE _____

ANIMAL (PLURAL) _____

VERB (PAST TENSE) _____

SOMETHING ALIVE _____

PART OF THE BODY _____

VERB _____

NOUN _____

NOUN _____

PERSON IN ROOM _____

LETTER OF THE ALPHABET _____

ADJECTIVE _____

OCCUPATION _____

ADJECTIVE _____

ARTICLE OF CLOTHING _____

NOUN _____

NUMBER _____

VERB _____

LESLIE AND BEN 4EVER

"I love you and I _____ you." Leslie says these _____
                    VERB   ADJECTIVE

words to Ben when they get married, but these two love-

_____ had a long path to becoming Pawnee's perfect
ANIMAL (PLURAL)

couple. When they first met, Leslie actually _____
                                              VERB (PAST TENSE)

Ben! She called him a/an _____ to his _____
                         SOMETHING ALIVE   PART OF THE BODY

when he arrived to _____ the budget. Over time, though,
                   VERB

the pair came to understand and respect each other, and they soon fell

in _____. But they had to keep their _____ secret
   NOUN   NOUN

due to _____'s rule against interoffice relationships. After a
       PERSON IN ROOM

lot of back and forth—and a Model U-_____ fiasco—
                                     LETTER OF THE ALPHABET

they came clean and made things _____. Ben went on to
                                ADJECTIVE

help Leslie win her campaign for City _____ before making
                                       OCCUPATION

the difficult choice to take a job in Washington, DC. Eventually, the

_____-distance relationship became too much for Ben—he
ADJECTIVE

surprised Leslie in Pawnee with an engagement _____!
                                               ARTICLE OF CLOTHING

They got married in _____ Hall and went on to have
                    NOUN

_____ children. Can you _____ #CoupleGoals?
NUMBER   VERB

MAD LIBS® is fun to play with friends, but you can also play it by yourself! To begin with, DO NOT look at the story on the page below. Fill in the blanks on this page with the words called for. Then, using the words you have selected, fill in the blank spaces in the story.

Now you've created your own hilarious MAD LIBS® game!

A TRAEGER TUESDAY

NOUN _____

ARTICLE OF CLOTHING (PLURAL) _____

VERB _____

ADJECTIVE _____

NUMBER _____

NOUN _____

VERB _____

NOUN _____

ADJECTIVE _____

VERB ENDING IN "ING" _____

NOUN _____

NUMBER _____

OCCUPATION _____

VERB ENDING IN "ING" _____

TYPE OF FOOD _____

EXCLAMATION _____

VERB _____

NOUN _____

A TRAEGER TUESDAY

Chris Traeger is Pawnee's most positive _____—what does
NOUN

a day in his _____ look like? _____
ARTICLE OF CLOTHING (PLURAL)   VERB

at his agenda for a typical Tuesday:

5:00 a.m.: Wake up after a whole five hours of _____ sleep.
ADJECTIVE

Go for a leisurely _____-mile run. Then eat breakfast! It is
NUMBER

literally the most important _____ of the day.
NOUN

8:55 a.m.: Arrive at work, ready to _____ the day with a
VERB

smile!

1:00 p.m.: Use my lunch _____ for another _____
NOUN   ADJECTIVE

run. Must keep _____ to avoid falling into the
VERB ENDING IN "ING"

bottomless _____ of despair.
NOUN

4:00 p.m.: Time for _____ hours of therapy with my
NUMBER

personal _____, Dr. Nygard, followed by _____
OCCUPATION   VERB ENDING IN "ING"

a hearty meal of vegetable loaf sweetened with _____
TYPE OF FOOD

reduction. _____!
EXCLAMATION

11:30 p.m.: _____ into bed after *literally* the best
VERB

_____ ever.
NOUN

MAD LIBS® is fun to play with friends, but you can also play it by yourself! To begin with, DO NOT look at the story on the page below. Fill in the blanks on this page with the words called for. Then, using the words you have selected, fill in the blank spaces in the story.

Now you've created your own hilarious MAD LIBS® game!

A NIGHT AT THE SNAKEHOLE LOUNGE

NOUN _____

ANIMAL _____

NOUN _____

ADJECTIVE _____

ADVERB _____

TYPE OF LIQUID _____

ADJECTIVE _____

NUMBER _____

ADJECTIVE _____

PLURAL NOUN _____

SILLY WORD _____

PERSON IN ROOM _____

VERB ENDING IN "ING" _____

ADJECTIVE _____

VEHICLE _____

NOUN _____

ADJECTIVE _____

NOUN _____

It was party time at the Snakehole Lounge, and everyone from the

Parks and _____ Department was having a blast! Tom had

NOUN

asked everybody to help him launch his new drink, _____-

ANIMAL

Juice, at Pawnee's sickest night-_____ . Although they were

NOUN

_____ about it at first, everyone _____ decided to

ADJECTIVE · ADVERB

come. They all tried out the _____-style liquor to help

TYPE OF LIQUID

promote the drink's high-end, _____ lifestyle. But within

ADJECTIVE

_____ minutes, the night took a turn for the _____!

NUMBER · ADJECTIVE

April and Andy were both pretending to be _____ that

PLURAL NOUN

they weren't, and Ben wouldn't stop saying "_____!"

SILLY WORD

_____ kept _____ the whole night! But

PERSON IN ROOM · VERB ENDING IN "ING"

worst of all, best friends Leslie and Ann got in a/an _____

ADJECTIVE

argument. Eventually, Donna had to drive the group home in her

_____ . The next day, everyone was feeling like

VEHICLE

_____ , but no one would ever forget their _____

NOUN · ADJECTIVE

night at the Snake-_____ Lounge!

NOUN

MAD LIBS® is fun to play with friends, but you can also play it by yourself! To begin with, DO NOT look at the story on the page below. Fill in the blanks on this page with the words called for. Then, using the words you have selected, fill in the blank spaces in the story.

Now you've created your own hilarious MAD LIBS® game!

INVITATION TO
THE HARVEST FESTIVAL

PERSON IN ROOM _____

ADVERB _____

NOUN _____

ADVERB _____

TYPE OF EVENT _____

VERB _____

NUMBER _____

TYPE OF FOOD _____

SILLY WORD _____

PLURAL NOUN _____

ANIMAL _____

ADJECTIVE _____

PART OF THE BODY _____

ADJECTIVE _____

CELEBRITY _____

ADJECTIVE _____

VERB _____

MAD LIBS®
INVITATION TO
THE HARVEST FESTIVAL

Parks and Recreation

Dear _____ ,
_____PERSON IN ROOM_____

You are _____ invited to what is sure to be the greatest
_____ADVERB_____

_____ in history, Pawnee's Harvest Festival! Everyone at the
_____NOUN_____

Parks Department has been working _____ to bring you the
_____ADVERB_____

best Harvest _____ since 1987. This weeklong festival has
_____TYPE OF EVENT_____

so much to _____ : over _____ carnival games,
_____VERB_____   _____NUMBER_____

southern Indiana's largest _____ maze, and a/an
_____TYPE OF FOOD_____

_____ wheel where you can see for twenty _____
_____SILLY WORD_____   _____PLURAL NOUN_____

at the top! Don't miss our musical act, _____ Rat, and check
_____ANIMAL_____

out _____ Fried Boulevard, where there's fried food as far as
_____ADJECTIVE_____

the _____ can see. Yum! And last but not least, don't miss
_____PART OF THE BODY_____

our _____ attraction—the one and only Li'l Sebastian!
_____ADJECTIVE_____

Sincerely,

_____
_____CELEBRITY_____

PS You may have heard about a/an _____ Wamapoke tribe
_____ADJECTIVE_____

curse on the festival's grounds, but we have it all under control. No

need to _____ !
_____VERB_____

MAD LIBS® is fun to play with friends, but you can also play it by yourself! To begin with, DO NOT look at the story on the page below. Fill in the blanks on this page with the words called for. Then, using the words you have selected, fill in the blank spaces in the story.

Now you've created your own hilarious MAD LIBS® game!

TREAT YO' SELF

NOUN _____

PLURAL NOUN _____

NOUN _____

ARTICLE OF CLOTHING (PLURAL) _____

ADJECTIVE _____

VERB _____

NUMBER _____

A PLACE _____

VERB _____

VERB _____

ANIMAL _____

ADJECTIVE _____

NUMBER _____

PART OF THE BODY _____

TYPE OF FOOD _____

ADJECTIVE _____

MAD LIBS

TREAT YO' SELF

It's the best day of the _____! Treat yo' self like Tom and

NOUN

Donna by following their list of dos and _____:

PLURAL NOUN

- DO treat yo' _____ to elegant cashmere

NOUN

  _____, plenty of mimosas, and of course,

ARTICLE OF CLOTHING (PLURAL)

  _____ leather goods.

ADJECTIVE

- DON'T skimp out! _____ Yo' Self day is about the

VERB

  finer things—who cares if you spend _____ dollars?

NUMBER

- DO be sure to go to a spa, the mall, and (the) _____.

A PLACE

  Allow the luxury to _____ over you.

VERB

- DON'T be afraid to _____ what you want, especially if

VERB

  it's a/an _____-man costume!

ANIMAL

- DO make time for some _____ acupuncture. Relaxation

ADJECTIVE

  Rule # _____: Needles in your _____,

NUMBER · PART OF THE BODY

  pleasure in yo' base.

- DON'T eat _____ alone on a bench. Ever. That's just

TYPE OF FOOD

  _____.

ADJECTIVE

MAD LIBS® is fun to play with friends, but you can also play it by yourself! To begin with, DO NOT look at the story on the page below. Fill in the blanks on this page with the words called for. Then, using the words you have selected, fill in the blank spaces in the story.

Now you've created your own hilarious MAD LIBS® game!

THE TROUBLE WITH TAMMYS

EXCLAMATION _____

VERB _____

PLURAL NOUN _____

NUMBER _____

TYPE OF FOOD _____

ADJECTIVE _____

TYPE OF BUILDING _____

FIRST NAME _____

OCCUPATION (PLURAL) _____

ADJECTIVE _____

A PLACE _____

NUMBER _____

EXCLAMATION _____

ARTICLE OF CLOTHING _____

TYPE OF CONTAINER _____

NOUN _____

MAD LIBS
THE TROUBLE
WITH TAMMYS

_____ , it's Tammy time! _____ your knowledge
  EXCLAMATION   VERB

of these three _____ from Ron's life—can you match the
             PLURAL NOUN

fact to either Tammy 0, Tammy 1, or Tammy _____?
                                   NUMBER

a) Which Tammy was a/an _____ striper at the
                      TYPE OF FOOD

   _____ hospital where Ron was born and was his Sunday
   ADJECTIVE

   _____ teacher?
   TYPE OF BUILDING

b) This _____ works at the library. Ew, _____ .
       FIRST NAME   OCCUPATION (PLURAL)

c) One of the Tammys is actually Ron's _____ mother—
                               ADJECTIVE

   which one is it?

d) This Tammy has a room in her _____ that is full of
                              A PLACE

   over _____ guns. _____!
           NUMBER   EXCLAMATION

e) Ron wears a red polo _____ after spending the
                       ARTICLE OF CLOTHING

   night with this Tammy.

f) Which Tammy threw a/an _____ of acid at Ron's
                        TYPE OF CONTAINER

   new girl-_____?
           NOUN

Answer key: (a) Tammy 1, (b) Tammy 2, (c) Tammy 0, (d) Tammy 0,

(e) Tammy 2, (f) Tammy 1

MAD LIBS® is fun to play with friends, but you can also play it by yourself! To begin with, DO NOT look at the story on the page below. Fill in the blanks on this page with the words called for. Then, using the words you have selected, fill in the blank spaces in the story.

Now you've created your own hilarious MAD LIBS® game!

COME TO RENT-A-SWAG!

VERB ENDING IN "ING" _____

NOUN _____

ADVERB _____

NOUN _____

VERB _____

VERB _____

PLURAL NOUN _____

ADJECTIVE _____

ARTICLE OF CLOTHING _____

NUMBER _____

NOUN _____

ARTICLE OF CLOTHING (PLURAL) _____

COLOR _____

NOUN _____

VERB ENDING IN "ING" _____

NOUN _____

ADJECTIVE _____

NOUN _____

MAD LIBS®

COME TO RENT-A-SWAG!

Are you a teen _____ for a swagalicious _____
        VERB ENDING IN "ING"   NOUN

for Homecoming? Is your mom worried you'll grow out of it too

_____? Looking for an affordable _____ to
        ADVERB   NOUN

all these problems? Well, _____ no further! Swing by
                                    VERB

_____ -A-Swag for all your fashion _____ .
        VERB   PLURAL NOUN

We're Pawnee's only _____ clothes rental service for
                            ADJECTIVE

teens, tweens, and everything in-betweens. Searching for a swanky

_____? We've got dozens of them, for just _____
ARTICLE OF CLOTHING   NUMBER

dollars a week! Hoping to impress the _____ in your life?
                                              NOUN

Check out our _____ —they come in black,
            ARTICLE OF CLOTHING (PLURAL)

blue, or _____ . One satisfied _____ even said,
            COLOR   NOUN

"I've saved so much money by _____ at Rent-A-Swag!"
                                VERB ENDING IN "ING"

So come on down to Rent-A/An- _____ for the dopest
                                        NOUN

clothes at the most _____ prices! *My name is Tom Haverford,*
                        ADJECTIVE

and I approve this _____ .
                        NOUN

MAD LIBS® is fun to play with friends, but you can also play it by yourself! To begin with, DO NOT look at the story on the page below. Fill in the blanks on this page with the words called for. Then, using the words you have selected, fill in the blank spaces in the story.

Now you've created your own hilarious MAD LIBS® game!

JOHNNY KARATE

ADJECTIVE _____

VERB ENDING IN "ING" _____

CELEBRITY _____

EXCLAMATION _____

FIRST NAME _____

NUMBER _____

VERB _____

ADJECTIVE _____

OCCUPATION _____

ANIMAL (PLURAL) _____

ADJECTIVE _____

PLURAL NOUN _____

SILLY WORD _____

VERB _____

NOUN _____

NOUN _____

ADJECTIVE _____

MAD LIBS®

Parks and Recreation

JOHNNY KARATE

It's the *Johnny Karate Super* _____ *Musical Explosion Show*!
                                    ADJECTIVE

In this episode, Johnny started off _____ the welcome
                                    VERB ENDING IN "ING"

song, only to realize that his framed _____ jersey had been
                                        CELEBRITY

stolen. _____! This looks like a job for _____
        EXCLAMATION   FIRST NAME

Macklin! With Macklin on the case, Johnny laid out his _____
                                                        NUMBER

Karate Moves to Success: make something, _____ something,
                                          VERB

karate-chop something, try something _____ even if
                                      ADJECTIVE

it's scary to you, and be nice to someone. Next, _____
                                                  OCCUPATION

Smartbrain taught everyone how to calculate how many

_____ could fit inside the missing jersey. *Bzzt!* Johnny
ANIMAL (PLURAL)

pushed the _____ Buzzer! Soon Mailman Barry arrived
            ADJECTIVE

with the _____ , then ninjas started attacking him.
          PLURAL NOUN

_____! Then, Leslie Knope helped Johnny face his fear of
SILLY WORD

2 percent milk by having him _____ a glass. Finally, Johnny
                              VERB

was nice to himself about not finding the missing _____ .
                                                    NOUN

Wait! It turns out Mailman Barry accidentally had the jersey in his

_____ -bag all along. _____ Barry!
NOUN   ADJECTIVE

MAD LIBS® is fun to play with friends, but you can also play it by yourself! To begin with, DO NOT look at the story on the page below. Fill in the blanks on this page with the words called for. Then, using the words you have selected, fill in the blank spaces in the story.

Now you've created your own hilarious MAD LIBS® game!

DEAR POETIC NOBLE LAND-MERMAID

ADJECTIVE _____

SOMETHING ALIVE _____

NUMBER _____

NOUN _____

PERSON IN ROOM _____

ADJECTIVE _____

NOUN _____

PLURAL NOUN _____

VERB _____

ADJECTIVE _____

ANIMAL _____

NOUN _____

PART OF THE BODY _____

PLURAL NOUN _____

NUMBER _____

EXCLAMATION _____

VERB _____

ADVERB _____

Dear Poetic _____ Land-_____,
            ADJECTIVE   SOMETHING ALIVE

Oh Ann, perfect sunflower Ann. I know Michigan is only _____
                                                     NUMBER

miles away from Pawnee, but it feels so much farther. You beautiful

unicorn _____, I hope you and _____ are doing
            NOUN   PERSON IN ROOM

well. I'm sure _____ baby Oliver is quite the handful, but I
                 ADJECTIVE

know that a/an _____-breaking moth like you can handle
                NOUN

anything. Oh, did my Ann Day _____ arrive yet? I know
                            PLURAL NOUN

we said to only send one gift, but I couldn't _____ myself!
                                      VERB

A talented, _____, powerful musk-_____
               ADJECTIVE   ANIMAL

like Ann Perkins deserves only the best! You are a kind and lovely

_____, and your brain is almost as perfect as your
           NOUN

_____ . I wish I could tell you these _____
     PART OF THE BODY   PLURAL NOUN

in person, but in place of that, I've included a list of _____
                                              NUMBER

more compliments on the back of this letter. _____, I just
                                        EXCLAMATION

_____ and miss you so much!
     VERB

_____,
   ADVERB

Leslie

MAD LIBS® is fun to play with friends, but you can also play it by yourself! To begin with, DO NOT look at the story on the page below. Fill in the blanks on this page with the words called for. Then, using the words you have selected, fill in the blank spaces in the story.

Now you've created your own hilarious MAD LIBS® game!

DUNSHIRE OR DUNCE?

NOUN _____

VERB _____

ADJECTIVE _____

ARTICLE OF CLOTHING _____

EXCLAMATION _____

VERB _____

ADJECTIVE _____

VERB _____

NUMBER _____

PLURAL NOUN _____

ADVERB _____

PLURAL NOUN _____

ADVERB _____

COLOR _____

VERB (PAST TENSE) _____

ADJECTIVE _____

PLURAL NOUN _____

Parks and Recreation

MAD LIBS®

DUNSHIRE OR DUNCE?

Enter the _____ of the Cones of Dunshire! _____

NOUN   VERB

this quiz to find out if you're a novice or a natural:

1. Besides wearing the _____ _____,

ADJECTIVE   ARTICLE OF CLOTHING

   what's the Ledgerman's role?

   (a) They keep score, _____!

EXCLAMATION

   (b) They _____ on a ledge.

VERB

2. True or _____ : You only use three dice.

ADJECTIVE

   (a) False—you _____ three dice to see how many dice

VERB

   you roll with (up to _____!).

NUMBER

   (b) True—how many more six-sided _____ do you

PLURAL NOUN

   _____ need?

ADVERB

3. What's the true essence of the _____ of Dunshire?

PLURAL NOUN

   (a) Duh, it's _____ about the cones!

ADVERB

   (b) Uh . . . the _____ tiles . . . ?

COLOR

If you _____ mostly *a*'s, you're almost as smart as the

VERB (PAST TENSE)

_____ Architect! Mostly *b*'s means you may need to brush

ADJECTIVE

up on your Dunshire _____ .

PLURAL NOUN

MAD LIBS® is fun to play with friends, but you can also play it by yourself! To begin with, DO NOT look at the story on the page below. Fill in the blanks on this page with the words called for. Then, using the words you have selected, fill in the blank spaces in the story.

Now you've created your own hilarious MAD LIBS® game!

ENTERTAINMENT 720

PERSON IN ROOM _____

FIRST NAME _____

NOUN _____

NOUN _____

CELEBRITY _____

ANIMAL _____

ADJECTIVE _____

NUMBER _____

ADJECTIVE _____

VERB _____

OCCUPATION (PLURAL) _____

ADJECTIVE _____

SILLY WORD _____

ADJECTIVE _____

TYPE OF FOOD (PLURAL) _____

VERB _____

PLURAL NOUN _____

EXCLAMATION _____

Wassup, _____ , it's ya boys Tom and _____ -Ralphio!
       PERSON IN ROOM   FIRST NAME

Welcome to Entertainment 720, where we're willing to go around the

_____ twice for our clients. If at any time you want to play
     NOUN

_____ with professional basketball player _____ or
     NOUN   CELEBRITY

pet a wild Bengal _____ , go right ahead. And don't forget
                        ANIMAL

to grab a/an _____ iPad whenever you want. Here at
                  ADJECTIVE

Entertainment _____ , life is one giant _____
                    NUMBER   ADJECTIVE

party. Seriously—_____ that button to play some sick
                        VERB

tunes and dance with all the _____ we hired. Want
                                   OCCUPATION (PLURAL)

some _____ champagne in a gold-plated glass? We got it.
         ADJECTIVE

_____ d'oeuvres? We got those, too! Feel like the very
   SILLY WORD

_____ person you are in one of our three different VIP
   ADJECTIVE

areas—each one has its own bar and a wall of _____ .
                                                 TYPE OF FOOD (PLURAL)

How do we _____ money, you ask? By printing our own
               VERB

_____ of course! At E-720, we've got it all. Oh, what's
   PLURAL NOUN

that? We just went bankrupt? _____ !
                                 EXCLAMATION

MAD LIBS® is fun to play with friends, but you can also play it by yourself! To begin with, DO NOT look at the story on the page below. Fill in the blanks on this page with the words called for. Then, using the words you have selected, fill in the blank spaces in the story.

Now you've created your own hilarious MAD LIBS® game!

THE SWANSON PYRAMID OF GREATNESS

NOUN _____

ADJECTIVE _____

ADJECTIVE _____

CELEBRITY _____

ADJECTIVE _____

NUMBER _____

VERB ENDING IN "ING" _____

ANIMAL _____

VERB _____

ADJECTIVE _____

NOUN _____

OCCUPATION _____

ADJECTIVE _____

NUMBER _____

VERB _____

TYPE OF LIQUID _____

Ron's perfectly calculated _____ for maximum _____
                                      NOUN   ADJECTIVE

achievement has a lot of insight to bestow. Check out some of the

_____ highlights:
ADJECTIVE

- **Capitalism:** _____'s way of determining who is smart
                              CELEBRITY

  and who is _____ .
                  ADJECTIVE

- **Friends:** One to _____ is sufficient.
                          NUMBER

- _____ : Acceptable at funerals and the Grand
  VERB ENDING IN "ING"

  Canyon.

- **Poise:** Sting like a/an _____ . Do not _____
                                      ANIMAL   VERB

  like a butterfly. That's _____ .
                                ADJECTIVE

- **Cursing:** There's only one bad _____ : taxes. If any
                                          NOUN

  other word is good enough for a/an _____ , it's
                                            OCCUPATION

  _____ enough for you.
  ADJECTIVE

- **Rage:** One rage every _____ months is permitted. Try
                                NUMBER

  not to _____ anyone who doesn't deserve it.
            VERB

- **Skim** _____ : Avoid it.
            TYPE OF LIQUID

MAD LIBS® is fun to play with friends, but you can also play it by yourself! To begin with, DO NOT look at the story on the page below. Fill in the blanks on this page with the words called for. Then, using the words you have selected, fill in the blank spaces in the story.

Now you've created your own hilarious MAD LIBS® game!

APRIL OR ANDY?

ADJECTIVE _____

NOUN _____

ANIMAL _____

PLURAL NOUN _____

NUMBER _____

NOUN _____

TYPE OF LIQUID _____

ANIMAL _____

NOUN _____

ADJECTIVE _____

NOUN _____

FIRST NAME _____

ADJECTIVE _____

LETTER OF THE ALPHABET _____

ADJECTIVE _____

ADJECTIVE _____

NOUN _____

APRIL OR ANDY?

April and Andy are one of Pawnee's most _____ couples.

ADJECTIVE

Which _____ are you more like?

NOUN

1. Are you more of a cat person or a/an _____ person?

ANIMAL

    (a) Cat person—they like to hiss at _____ , like me.

PLURAL NOUN

    (b) Dog person—they're so happy, especially _____ -legged

NUMBER

    dogs like Champion!

2. What's your all- _____ favorite band?

NOUN

    (a) Neutral _____ Hotel

TYPE OF LIQUID

    (b) Mouse _____ , duh! Best _____ ever!

ANIMAL   NOUN

3. It's time for some _____ role-play! Describe your alter

ADJECTIVE

    _____ :

NOUN

    (a) I'm _____ Snakehole, a very _____ widow

FIRST NAME   ADJECTIVE

    with a terrible secret.

    (b) I'm Burt Macklin, FB- _____ .

LETTER OF THE ALPHABET

If you picked mostly *a*'s, you're as sarcastic and _____ as

ADJECTIVE

April. Mostly *b*'s means you're just as goofy and _____ as

ADJECTIVE

Pawnee's resident _____ -star Andy!

NOUN

MAD LIBS® is fun to play with friends, but you can also play it by yourself! To begin with, DO NOT look at the story on the page below. Fill in the blanks on this page with the words called for. Then, using the words you have selected, fill in the blank spaces in the story.

Now you've created your own hilarious MAD LIBS® game!

YA' HEARD? WITH PERD

NUMBER _____

VERB (PAST TENSE) _____

NOUN _____

SILLY WORD _____

EXCLAMATION _____

VERB ENDING IN "ING" _____

NOUN _____

VERB _____

ADJECTIVE _____

OCCUPATION _____

PLURAL NOUN _____

ADVERB _____

ANIMAL _____

PLURAL NOUN _____

NOUN _____

COUNTRY _____

ADJECTIVE _____

YA' HEARD? WITH PERD

Here is a transcript of episode number _____ of *Ya' Heard?*

NUMBER

With Perd:

Perd: Welcome to *Ya'* _____? *With Perd*. We're here with

VERB (PAST TENSE)

our _____ Annabel Porter, the CEO of _____.

NOUN

SILLY WORD

Annabel Porter: _____! It's me, I'm here.

EXCLAMATION

Perd: Let's begin the show by _____ it. Ms. Porter, my

VERB ENDING IN "ING"

_____ for you is, Why are you here?

NOUN

Annabel: Well, Perd, I'm here to _____ this month's

VERB

_____ trends.

ADJECTIVE

Perd: And because you are a lifestyle _____ and trendsetter,

OCCUPATION

what _____ are you setting?

PLURAL NOUN

Annabel: My must-have are these _____ audacious

ADVERB

_____ milk coattails. All-natural manufactured

ANIMAL

_____ are making a comeback, too. And of course,

PLURAL NOUN

gluten-free _____ drops are the new _____

NOUN

COUNTRY

throw pillows.

Perd: Those items do in fact sound _____!

ADJECTIVE

MAD LIBS® is fun to play with friends, but you can also play it by yourself! To begin with, DO NOT look at the story on the page below. Fill in the blanks on this page with the words called for. Then, using the words you have selected, fill in the blank spaces in the story.

Now you've created your own hilarious MAD LIBS® game!

GARRY, JERRY, LARRY, OR TERRY?

NOUN _____

FIRST NAME _____

PLURAL NOUN _____

NOUN _____

OCCUPATION _____

ADJECTIVE _____

VERB ENDING IN "ING" _____

A PLACE _____

CITY _____

NOUN _____

VERB (PAST TENSE) _____

NUMBER _____

PERSON IN ROOM _____

ADVERB _____

ADJECTIVE _____

NOUN _____

VERB _____

Oh, hi there! My _____ is Garry Gergich, but you can call
NOUN

me _____ . I've actually gone by many names over the
FIRST NAME

_____ . I love my _____ at the Parks Department,
PLURAL NOUN NOUN

but on my first day on the job, the _____ called me
OCCUPATION

"Jerry." Well, I guess I was too _____ to correct him, so
ADJECTIVE

everyone just kept _____ me Jerry. Eventually I retired,
VERB ENDING IN "ING"

only to come back once again to (the) _____ to help with
A PLACE

the _____/Eagleton merger. I wanted a fresh _____ ,
CITY NOUN

but I got too gosh-darn confused and I _____ myself
VERB (PAST TENSE)

"Larry" by mistake. This time, that name didn't last long . . . but that

was because _____ years later they all started calling me
NUMBER

"Terry" instead. Thankfully, at _____ 's wedding, she
PERSON IN ROOM

_____ wrote my name as "Garry" on the invitation, and I
ADVERB

was back to my _____ name again! Anyway . . . I'll be
ADJECTIVE

honest, I'm not sure how to end this _____—no one ever
NOUN

lets me _____ this long!
VERB

MAD LIBS® is fun to play with friends, but you can also play it by yourself! To begin with, DO NOT look at the story on the page below. Fill in the blanks on this page with the words called for. Then, using the words you have selected, fill in the blank spaces in the story.

Now you've created your own hilarious MAD LIBS® game!

PERKINS'S PAST PARTNERS

LAST NAME _____

ADJECTIVE _____

ADJECTIVE _____

FIRST NAME _____

VERB ENDING IN "ING" _____

PART OF THE BODY (PLURAL) _____

VERB (PAST TENSE) _____

ADVERB _____

ADVERB _____

EXCLAMATION _____

LAST NAME _____

ADJECTIVE _____

ADJECTIVE _____

VERB (PAST TENSE) _____

NOUN _____

PLURAL NOUN _____

NOUN _____

MAD LIBS®

Parks and Recreation

PERKINS'S PAST PARTNERS

Ann _____ has had her share of _____ relationships,
LAST NAME   ADJECTIVE

both good and _____ . Here are some highlights:
ADJECTIVE

- _____ **Dwyer:** Yes, before Andy found April, he
  FIRST NAME

  was _____ Ann! But when he lied about his
  VERB ENDING IN "ING"

  _____ still being broken, the pair split.
  PART OF THE BODY (PLURAL)

- **Mark Brendanawicz:** Ann started dating Mark after Leslie

  _____ Ann that she was _____ over him.
  VERB (PAST TENSE)   ADVERB

  Mark almost proposed, but instead she _____ broke up
  ADVERB

  with him. _____!
  EXCLAMATION

- **Tom** _____ : Tom made Ann laugh and had
  LAST NAME

  _____ blankets, but they were a truly _____ pair.
  ADJECTIVE   ADJECTIVE

- **Howard Tuttleman:** The less _____ about him,
  VERB (PAST TENSE)

  the better.

- **Chris Traeger:** The one and only _____ for Ann. They
  NOUN

  had their ups and _____ , but they are genuinely the
  PLURAL NOUN

  perfect _____ .
  NOUN

MAD LIBS® is fun to play with friends, but you can also play it by yourself! To begin with, DO NOT look at the story on the page below. Fill in the blanks on this page with the words called for. Then, using the words you have selected, fill in the blank spaces in the story.

Now you've created your own hilarious MAD LIBS® game!

GET ON YOUR FEET!

ADJECTIVE _____

NOUN _____

VERB _____

PART OF THE BODY (PLURAL) _____

VERB _____

CELEBRITY _____

ADVERB _____

FIRST NAME _____

ADJECTIVE _____

NOUN _____

NOUN _____

ADVERB _____

NOUN _____

NUMBER _____

VERB (PAST TENSE) _____

NOUN _____

NOUN _____

GET ON YOUR FEET!

Leslie Knope had a pretty _____ campaign to get elected to
                          ADJECTIVE

Pawnee's City _____ . Let's _____ at the most
                  NOUN   VERB

memorable moments:

- **Get on Your** _____: Leslie's team tried to
                  PART OF THE BODY (PLURAL)

  _____ her a rally where _____ would also
       VERB   CELEBRITY

  dunk a basketball, but everything seemed to go _____ .
                                                      ADVERB

- **Campaign Shake-Up:** Leslie hired her boyfriend _____
                                                       FIRST NAME

  to run her campaign, where he went up against a/an _____
                                                          ADJECTIVE

  opponent: Bobby Newport's _____ manager.
                                NOUN

- **Childhood** _____ **Ad:** The team posted a/an
                    NOUN

  _____ received ad online featuring a short
          ADVERB

  _____ of Leslie from when she was _____
       NOUN   NUMBER

  years old!

- **Debate Debacle:** Leslie _____ against her fellow
                              VERB (PAST TENSE)

  candidates, and after a rocky _____ , she crushed the
                                    NOUN

  competition.

- **Election Night:** Well, we all know how this _____ ended!
                                                    NOUN

MAD LIBS® is fun to play with friends, but you can also play it by yourself! To begin with, DO NOT look at the story on the page below. Fill in the blanks on this page with the words called for. Then, using the words you have selected, fill in the blank spaces in the story.

Now you've created your own hilarious MAD LIBS® game!

THE WOOOORST

ADJECTIVE _____

NOUN _____

LAST NAME _____

OCCUPATION _____

VERB _____

ADJECTIVE _____

NOUN _____

OCCUPATION _____

NUMBER _____

VERB ENDING IN "ING" _____

EXCLAMATION _____

NOUN _____

PLURAL NOUN _____

ADVERB _____

NOUN _____

COUNTRY _____

Pawnee has its fair share of _____ people, but Jean-Ralphio
<u>ADJECTIVE</u>

and Mona-Lisa Saperstein are definitely the woooorst. Jean-Ralphio

and his "twin sister from the same _____" are usually
<u>NOUN</u>

supported by their father, Dr. _____. He's a/an
<u>LAST NAME</u>

_____, so they usually _____ him for "Money,
<u>OCCUPATION</u>   <u>VERB</u>

please!" in order to get whatever they want. The pair were almost

partners with the _____ business Rent-A-Swag, but
<u>ADJECTIVE</u>

Jean-Ralphio got kicked off the _____. However, the
<u>NOUN</u>

Sapersteins still got to be involved when Tom hired Mona-Lisa as a/an

_____. Although she logged maybe _____
<u>OCCUPATION</u>   <u>NUMBER</u>

hours of work, she did end up _____ Tom for a while.
<u>VERB ENDING IN "ING"</u>

_____! It's no wonder Jean-Ralphio describes her as the
<u>EXCLAMATION</u>

"worst _____ in the world." But the _____ still
<u>NOUN</u>   <u>PLURAL NOUN</u>

stuck together. Until Jean-Ralphio _____ died . . . Just
<u>ADVERB</u>

kidding! He faked his own _____ so Mona-Lisa could collect
<u>NOUN</u>

his life-insurance money and they could move to _____
<u>COUNTRY</u>

forever!

MAD LIBS® is fun to play with friends, but you can also play it by yourself! To begin with, DO NOT look at the story on the page below. Fill in the blanks on this page with the words called for. Then, using the words you have selected, fill in the blank spaces in the story.

Now you've created your own hilarious MAD LIBS® game!

A TASTE OF PAWNEE

ADJECTIVE _____

NUMBER _____

PLURAL NOUN _____

ADJECTIVE _____

TYPE OF LIQUID _____

TYPE OF FOOD (PLURAL) _____

NUMBER _____

TYPE OF LIQUID _____

NOUN _____

NOUN _____

FIRST NAME _____

ADJECTIVE _____

TYPE OF BUILDING _____

SAME ADJECTIVE _____

ADVERB _____

NOUN _____

VERB _____

A TASTE OF PAWNEE

Pawnee has so many _____ food choices to explore, with
             ADJECTIVE

over _____ restaurants to experience! Check out some of the
     NUMBER

best _____ to try:
   PLURAL NOUN

- **The world-_____ waffles at JJ's Diner:** Topped with
          ADJECTIVE

  whipped _____ , these _____ from
       TYPE OF LIQUID   TYPE OF FOOD (PLURAL)

  JJ's Diner are the best in the world . . . or at least in Pawnee.

- **Fountain soda at Paunch Burger:** Coming in at _____
              NUMBER

  ounces, Paunch Burger's child-size _____ is roughly
          TYPE OF LIQUID

  the size of a two-year-old _____ if they were liquefied.
        NOUN

  At $1.59, it's a/an _____!
       NOUN

- **Porterhouse at _____ Mulligan's Steakhouse:**
         FIRST NAME

  According to Ron Swanson, this is the best _____
            ADJECTIVE

  porter-_____ in the _____ state.
     TYPE OF BUILDING   SAME ADJECTIVE

  _____ worth the trip!
    ADVERB

- **Mini calzones:** This is the one _____ on this list that
          NOUN

  you should *not* eat under any circumstances. _____ away!
             VERB

MAD LIBS® is fun to play with friends, but you can also play it by yourself! To begin with, DO NOT look at the story on the page below. Fill in the blanks on this page with the words called for. Then, using the words you have selected, fill in the blank spaces in the story.

Now you've created your own hilarious MAD LIBS® game!

ODE TO LI'L SEBASTIAN

CITY _____

NUMBER _____

ANIMAL _____

ADJECTIVE _____

ADJECTIVE _____

TYPE OF FOOD _____

VERB _____

ADJECTIVE _____

ADJECTIVE _____

NOUN _____

NUMBER _____

VERB _____

PART OF THE BODY _____

PLURAL NOUN _____

ADJECTIVE _____

VERB (PAST TENSE) _____

NUMBER _____

TYPE OF FOOD _____

MAD LIBS®

ODE TO LI'L SEBASTIAN

In the city of _____ , only _____ things unite us.
　　　　　　　　　CITY　　　　　　　　　　　　NUMBER

There's one miniature _____ we all idolize.
　　　　　　　　　　　　　ANIMAL

He's _____ and cute, with a/an _____ prance.
　　　ADJECTIVE　　　　　　　　　　　　　　　ADJECTIVE

It's Li'l Sebastian, the _____ of our eyes.
　　　　　　　　　　　　TYPE OF FOOD

His mane would _____ in the _____ morning sun,
　　　　　　　　　VERB　　　　　　　　　　ADJECTIVE

His hooves were the most _____ of forces.
　　　　　　　　　　　　　ADJECTIVE

Li'l Sebastian's story is one of triumph and _____ ,
　　　　　　　　　　　　　　　　　　　　　　NOUN

Plus, he sired over _____ minihorses.
　　　　　　　　　　　NUMBER

Li'l Sebastian could make a grown man _____
　　　　　　　　　　　　　　　　　　　　　VERB

Or a child's _____ light up with joy.
　　　　　PART OF THE BODY

It didn't matter that he had diabetes or _____ ,
　　　　　　　　　　　　　　　　　　　　PLURAL NOUN

Because that horse was one _____ boy.
　　　　　　　　　　　　　　ADJECTIVE

Though you may now be gone, we have not _____ .
　　　　　　　　　　　　　　　　　　VERB (PAST TENSE)

We will always remember you ideally.

For in heaven you can do your _____ favorite things:
　　　　　　　　　　　　　　　　NUMBER

Eating _____ and urinating freely.
　　　TYPE OF FOOD

From PARKS AND RECREATION MAD LIBS® • Parks and Recreation © 2021 Universal Television LLC.
All Rights Reserved. Published by Mad Libs, an imprint of Penguin Random House LLC.

Join the millions of Mad Libs fans creating wacky and wonderful stories on our apps!

Download Mad Libs today!